KENA UPANISHAD

De-gendering Hinduism.

Series Editor: Tapati Bharadwaj.

Published by

LIES AND BIG FEET

ISBN: 938428100X
ISBN-13: 978-9384281007

PREFATORY NOTE:

This rendition of an Upanishadic text is but a part of a larger series; the aim of this work is to construe Hindu religious texts as literature, and examine them within a gendered inflected analytical framework. What prevents us from examining the Upanishadic or the Vedic texts within a literary or a gendered perspective? If the basis of religion is "revealed knowledge," which was made evident to men – then is it not obvious that these notions of the Absolute Being would but be defined within gender inflected terminologies? The personal gender-biases of men would affect and predetermine how the notions of the Supreme Being were written about.

Let me explain with an example from an Upanishad. In the Aitareya Upanishad, the first stanza reads in the following manner:

"Om! In the beginning this was but the Absolute Self alone. There was nothing else whatsoever that winked. It thought, 'Let Me create the world.'"

We have to keep in mind that the Vedic texts are partially truthful – they are correct in their explanations on the notion of Absolute Consciousness which becomes matter, and there is no gender ascribed to this Absolute Being. The "Absolute Self" is denoted within gender neutral terms and is referred to as "It."

But there is a slippage which occurs in the Vedic texts, making these texts suspect: it reveals the fact that those who were writing about this kind of revealed, divine knowledge were men and their interests are evident in how the notion of Absolute Consciousness is defined and described. In the same Vedic text, we will find gender specific characteristics of the Absolute Being. The second stanza of the Aitreya Upanishad reads in the following manner:

"He created these worlds, viz. *ambhas, marici, mara* and *apah*. That which is beyond heaven is *ambhas*. Heaven is its support. The sky is *marici*. The earth is *mara*. The worlds that are below are the *apah*."

A shift occurs whereby, "It" becomes "He": and we all assume, and accept, that the Absolute Being has to be male. To follow this statement to its conclusion, we can state that as the Vedic texts equate the "Absolute Self" with the masculine, men are seen as being agents; in the second part of the Aitreya Upanishad, the first stanza reads: "In man indeed is the soul first conceived"; the implication is that men are agents in determining the birth of children while women are mere passive receptacles.

Biological sciences make use of these dichotomies, and feminists have critiqued how biology (which should be an objective science) makes use of the dominant trope of the "passive" female egg and the "active" male sperm. It is a notion that has also been used since times immemorial in the western worlds, beginning with Aristotle and St. Thomas.

There is no attempt by any religious institution to undress these entrenched misogyny that exists in Hinduism; and these dominant mainstream institutions simply reiterate the status quo. If we pick up a random text on religion that has been published by a well-recognized, religious institution, like the Ramakrishna Mission (that is seen as epitomising modern Hinduism), we find a similar trope operating as the subtext.

In <u>How is a man Reborn,</u> a short text that was published in 1970, by Advaita Ashrama, the publishing house of the Ramakrishna Mission, Swami Satprakashananda makes use of the same above mentioned dichotomy (pp.43-48); he cites instances from the <u>Chandogya Upanishad,</u> the <u>Brhadaranyaka Upanishad,</u> one Dr. Sturtevant, the <u>Aitareya Upanishad</u> and Sankara to prove the same point, whereby women are seen as passive agents whose only role in society is to procreate while men and sons do all the active work.

We can but make a beginning in dismantling these texts on Hinduism by re-transcribing them. The hope is that our daughters will be able to live in a gender –neutral society.

NEW VERSION OF THE KENA UPANISHAD

THE ARRANGEMENT OF THE TEXT:

ON THE LEFT SIDE, THERE IS THE OLDER VERSION OF THE **KENA UPANISHAD** AND THE RIGHT SIDE HAS A REVISED VERSION OF THE TEXT.

KENA UPANISHAD.

PART I

1. Willed by whom does the directed mind go towards its object? Being directed by whom does the vital force that precedes all, proceed (towards its duty)? By whom is this speech willed that people utter? Who is the effulgent being who directs the eyes and the ears?.

1. Willed by whom does the directed mind go towards its object? Being directed by whom does the vital force that precedes all, proceed (towards its duty)? By whom is this speech willed that people utter? Who is the effulgent being who directs the eyes and the ears?.

2. Since He is the ear, the Mind of the mind, the Speech of speech, the Life of life, and the Eye of the eye, therefore the intelligent men after giving up (self-identification with the senses) and renouncing this world, become immortal.

2. Since S/he is the ear, the Mind of the mind, the Speech of speech, the Life of life, and the Eye of the eye, therefore the intelligent person after giving up (self-identification with the senses) and renouncing this world, become immortal.

3. The eye does not go there, nor speech, nor mind. We do not know (Brahman to be such and such); hence we are not aware of any process of instructing about It.

3. The eye does not go there, nor speech, nor mind. We do not know (Brahman to be such and such); hence we are not aware of any process of instructing about It.

4. "That (Brahman) is surely different from the known; and again, It is above the unknown" – such was (the utterance) we heard of the ancient (teachers) who explained It to us.

4. "That (Brahman) is surely different from the known; and again, It is above the unknown" – such was (the utterance) we heard of the ancient (teachers) who explained It to us.

5. That which is not uttered by speech, that by which speech is revealed, know that alone to be Brahman, and not what people worship as an object.

5. That which is not uttered by speech, that by which speech is revealed, know that alone to be Brahman, and not what people worship as an object.

6. That which man does not comprehend with the mind, that by which, they say, the mind is encompassed, know that to be Brahman and not what people worship as an object.

6. That which a person does not comprehend with the mind, that by which, they say, the mind is encompassed, know that to be Brahman and not what people worship as an object.

7. That which man does not see
   with the eye, that by which
   man perceives the activities of
   the eye, know that alone to be
   Brahman and not what people
   worship as an object.

7. That which a person does not see with the eye, that by which s/he perceives the activities of the eye, know that alone to be Brahman and not what people worship as an object.

8. That which man does not hear with the ear, that by which man knows this ear, know that to be Brahman and not this that people worship as an object.

8. That which a person does not hear with the ear, that by which s/he knows this ear, know that to be Brahman and not this that people worship as an object.

9. That which man does not smell with the organ of smell, that by which the organ of smell is impelled, know that to be Brahman and not what people worship as an object.

9. That which a person does not smell with the organ of smell, that by which the organ of smell is impelled, know that to be Brahman and not what people worship as an object.

PART II

1. (Teacher): 'If you think, "I have known Brahman well enough," then you have known only the very little expression that It has in the human body and the little expression that It has among the gods. Therefore Brahman is still to be deliberated on by you.' (Disciple): I think (Brahman) is known.'

1. (Teacher): 'If you think, "I have known Brahman well enough," then you have known only the very little expression that It has in the human body and the little expression that It has among the Divine Beings. Therefore Brahman is still to be deliberated on by you.' (Disciple): I think (Brahman) is known.'

2. 'I do not think, "I know (Brahman) well enough": (i.e. I consider) "Not that I do not know; I know and I do not know as well." He among us who understands that utterance, "Not that I do not know; I know and I do not know as well", knows that (Brahman).'

2. 'I do not think, "I know (Brahman) well enough": (i.e. I consider) "Not that I do not know; I know and I do not know as well." S/he among us who understands that utterance, "Not that I do not know; I know and I do not know as well", knows that (Brahman).'

3. It is known to him to whom It
    is unknown; he does not
    know to whom It is known.
    It is unknown to those who
    know well, and known to
    those who do not know.

3.   It is known to that
     person to whom It is
     unknown; s/he does not
     know to whom It is
     known. It is unknown to
     those who know well,
     and known to those who
     do not know.

4. It (i.e. Brahman) is really known when It is known with (i.e. as the Self of) each state of consciousness, because thereby one gets immortality. (Since) through one's own Self is acquired strength, (therefore) through knowledge is attained immortality.

4. It (i.e. Brahman) is really known when It is known with (i.e. as the Self of) each state of consciousness, because thereby one gets immortality. (Since) through one's own Self is acquired strength, (therefore) through knowledge is attained immortality.

5. If one has realized here, then there is truth; if he has not realized here, then there is great destruction. The wise ones, having realized (Brahman) in all beings, and having turned away from this world, become immortal.

5.   If one has realized here, then there is truth; if s/he has not realized here, then there is great destruction. The wise ones, having realized (Brahman) in all beings, and having turned away from this world, become immortal.

PART III

1. It was Brahman, indeed, that achieved victory for the sake of the gods. In that victory which was in fact Brahman's, the gods became elated.

1. It was Brahman, indeed, that achieved victory for the sake of the Divine Beings. In that victory which was in fact Brahman's, the Divine Beings became elated.

2. They thought, 'Ours, indeed, is this victory, ours, indeed, is this glory,' Brahman knew this pretension of theirs. To them It did appear. They could not make out about that thing, as to what this Yaksa (venerable Being) might be.

2. They thought, 'Ours, indeed, is this victory, ours, indeed, is this glory,' Brahman knew this pretension of theirs. To them It did appear. They could not make out about that thing, as to what this Yaksa (venerable Being) might be.

3. They said to Fire, 'O
    Játavedá, find out thoroughly
    about this thing as to what
    this Yaksa is.' He said, 'So
    be it.'

3. They said to Fire, 'O
    Játavedá, find out
    thoroughly about this thing
    as to what this Yaksa is.'
    S/he said, 'So be it.'

4. To It he went. To him It said,
   'Who are you?' He said, 'I
   am known as Fire, or I am
   Játavedá,'

4. To It s/he went. To the person, It said, 'Who are you?' S/he said, 'I am known as Fire, or I am Játavedá,'

5. (It said), 'What power is there in you, such as you are?'
    (Fire said), 'I can burn up all this that is on the earth.'

5. (It said), 'What power is there in you, such as you are?' (Fire said), 'I can burn up all this that is on the earth.'

6. (Yaksa) placed a straw for him saying, 'Burn this.' (Fire) approached the straw with the power born of full enthusiasm. He could not consume it. He returned from the Yaksa (to tell the gods), ' I could not ascertain It fully as to what this Yaksa is.'

6. (Yaksa) placed a straw for the person saying, 'Burn this.' (Fire) approached the straw with the power born of full enthusiasm. S/he could not consume it. S/he returned from the Yaksa (to tell the Divine Beings), ' I could not ascertain It fully as to what this Yaksa is.'

7. Then (the gods) said to Air, 'O Air, find out thoroughly about this thing as to what this Yaksa is.' (Air said), 'So be it.'

7. Then (the Divine Beings) said to Air, 'O Air, find out thoroughly about this thing as to what this Yaksa is.' (Air said), 'So be it.'

8. To It he went. To him It said,
'Who are you?' He said, 'I
am known as Air, as I am
Mátariśvá.'

8. To It s/he went. To Air It
    said, 'Who are you?' S/he
    said, 'I am known as Air, as
    I am Mátariśvá.'

9. (It said), 'What power is there in you, such as you are?' (Air said), 'I can blow away all this that is on the earth.'

9. (It said), 'What power is there in you, such as you are?' (Air said), 'I can blow away all this that is on the earth.'

10. (Yaksa) placed a straw for him saying, 'Take it up.' Air approached the straw with all the strength born of enthusiasm. He could not take it up. He returned from that Yaksa (to tell the gods), 'I could not ascertain It fully as to what this Yaksa is.'

10. (Yaksa) placed a straw for Air saying, 'Take it up.' Air approached the straw with all the strength born of enthusiasm. S/he could not take it up. S/he returned from that Yaksa (to tell the Divine Beings), 'I could not ascertain It fully as to what this Yaksa is.'

11. Then (the gods) said to Indra, 'O Maghavá, find out thoroughly about this thing, as to what this Yaksa is.' (He said), 'So be it.' He (Indra) approached It (Yaksa). From him (Yaksa) vanished away.

11. Then (the gods) said to Indra, 'O Maghavá, find out thoroughly about this thing, as to what this Yaksa is.' (S/he said), 'So be it.' S/he (Indra) approached It (Yaksa). From Indra (Yaksa) vanished away.

12. In that very space he approached her, the superbly charming woman, viz. Umá Haimavatí. To Her (he said), 'What is this Yaksa?'

12. In that very space Indra
    approached a person, the
    superbly charming person,
    viz. Umá Haimavatí. To
    Her/ Him (s/he said), 'What
    is this Yaksa?'

PART IV

1. 'It was Brahman', said She. 'In Brahman's victory, you became elated thus.' From that (utterance) alone, to be sure, did Indra learn that It was Brahman.

1. 'It was Brahman', said S/he. 'In Brahman's victory, you became elated thus.' From that (utterance) alone, to be sure, did Indra learn that It was Brahman.

2. Therefore, indeed, these gods, viz. Fire, Air, and Indra, did excel other gods, for they indeed touched It most proximately, and they knew It first as Brahman.

2. Therefore, indeed, these
   Divine Beings, viz. Fire, Air,
   and Indra, did excel other
   Divine Beings, for they
   indeed touched It most
   proximately, and they knew
   It first as Brahman.

3. Therefore, did Indra excel the other deities. For he touched It most proximately, inasmuch as he knew It first as Brahman.

3. Therefore, did Indra excel the other deities. For s/he touched It most proximately, inasmuch as s/he knew It first as Brahman.

4. This is Its instruction (about meditation) through analogy. It is like that which is (known as) the flash of lightning, and It is also as though the eye winked. These are (illustrations) in a divine context.

4. This is Its instruction (about meditation) through analogy. It is like that which is (known as) the flash of lightning, and It is also as though the eye winked. These are (illustrations) in a divine context.

5. Then is the instruction
through analogy in the
context of the (individual)
self: This known fact, that
the mind seems to go to It
(Brahman), and the fact that
It (Brahman) is repeatedly
remembered through the
mind; as also the thought,
(that the mind has with
regard to Brahman).

5. Then is the instruction through analogy in the context of the (individual) self: This known fact, that the mind seems to go to It (Brahman), and the fact that It (Brahman) is repeatedly remembered through the mind; as also the thought, (that the mind has with regard to Brahman).

6. The Brahman is well known as the one adorable to all creatures: (hence) It is to be meditated on with the help of the name *tadvana*. All creatures surely pray to anyone who meditates on It in this way.

6. The Brahman is well known as the one adorable to all creatures: (hence) It is to be meditated on with the help of the name *tadvana*. All creatures surely pray to anyone who meditates on It in this way.

7. (Disciple: 'Sir, speak of the secret knowledge.'
    (Teacher): 'I have told you of the secret knowledge; I have imparted to you that very secret knowledge of Brahman.'

7. (Disciple: 'Ma'am/ Sir, speak of the secret knowledge.' (Teacher): 'I have told you of the secret knowledge; I have imparted to you that very secret knowledge of Brahman.'

8. Concentration, cessation from sense-objects, rites, etc. are its legs; the Vedas are all its limbs; truth is its abode.

8. Concentration, cessation from sense-objects, rites, etc. are its legs; the Vedas are all its limbs; truth is its abode.

9. Anyone who knows this thus, he, having dispelled sin, remains firmly seated in the boundless, blissful, and highest Brahman. He remains seated (there).

9. Anyone who knows this thus, s/he, having dispelled sin, remains firmly seated in the boundless, blissful, and highest Brahman. S/he remains seated (there).

ABOUT THE AUTHOR.

I grew up in an uber-brahmanical family where ritualistic worship was a part of my everyday life; the Vedic texts and the Upanishads were also something I grew up. I always thought that religion was something "out" there; I never actually thought that we were meant to believe in these texts on "revealed knowledge" in an absolute manner. But religion pervades every and all aspects of our lives – institutional, private or public, and be they secular, or not.

After reading the Hindu religious texts for myself, I realised how gendered these texts were, and to our sensibilities, the archaic notions that underlie the basic tenets of Hinduism sound ridiculous and perverse. We forget that the "revealed knowledge" that is evident in the Upanishads has been written by men, and their gender predetermined how they translated the notions of the Absolute Being into language.

I do not want my daughter to grow up within such a flawed belief system; we have to dismantle the existing religious texts as they are and re-transcribe them in order to arrive at gender-neutral concepts of religion, and Being.

www.ingramcontent.com/pod-product-compliance
Lightning Source LLC
Chambersburg PA
CBHW060652030426
42337CB00017B/2573